Morsels of Truth
Live, Love & Laugh in the Lord

A 60-Day Devotional Journal

First Edition

Sylvia Grimes-Myrie

APS Publishing
www.weareaps.com

TABLE OF CONTENTS

DAY ONE: OUR AWESOME GOD

Let me start with Genesis 1:1-2 (NKJV): "In the beginning God created the heavens and the earth. The earth was without form, and void, and darkness was on the face of the deep, and the spirit of God was hovering over the face of the waters."

I ask you to take notice of God's introduction of Himself. There is no mention of His birth or origin, it's simply noted that God was self-existent, pre-existent. God created the heavens and the earth from nothing visible, omnipotent.

And who taught Him what or how to create anything?

Omniscient.

To hover, according to (Webster's Dictionary) is to linger about, wait near at hand.

What was the Spirit waiting for?

Genesis 1:3 (NKJV): "In the beginning was the word, and the word was with God, and the word was God.

God's Word is alive. Revelation 19:13 (NKJV) "He was clothed with a robe dipped in blood, and His name is The Word of God. Jesus is the word of God. God spoke the word (Jesus) and the Holy Spirit went to work and creation began.

What an awesome God we serve.

ACTIVITY

Jot down some awesome wonders that God has performed for you today.

Purpose: to remind yourself that you always have something for which to be grateful.

DAY TWO: HIS MIGHTY WORKS

I pray you have begun your day with the thought that all is well.

I hope you awakened with your senses tuned to the sounds of birds singing, visions of squirrels frolicking about, the feel of a nice cool breeze on your skin, and the smell of the crisp morning air.

Okay, maybe you don't have all that surrounding you, but it is available for you to enjoy.

When you look around in this great big universe of ours, I can't imagine not thinking of how amazing and awesome God is.

Psalm 8:3 (NJKV) "When I consider your heavens, the work of Your fingers, the moon and the stars which you have ordained".

The thought that your God, your Heavenly Father created all of this should make you stand in awe of who He is and all His mighty works.

Psalm 111:2 "The works of the Lord are great....."

Psalm 111:3 "His work is honorable and glorious, and His righteousness endures forever.

Today I'd like to suggest that you take time to appreciate all that God has created in the earth including mankind, not taking it for granted, but appreciating and being grateful for all of His creation. Let us praise and exalt the Lord for all He has done; He is certainly worthy of all praise.

DAY THREE: FOOD FOR THOUGHT

Here's a little food for thought:

The Lord God says in Revelation 22:13 (NKJV) "I am the Alpha and the Omega, the Beginning and the End, the First and the Last."

God Himself is the One who establishes and is in control of your beginning (birth) as well as your end (death). He has given you free will to make choices in between stages – your life's journey. He created you with a purpose and a plan that will lead you to your purpose, yet so many go years trying to find their purpose in life.

Years of making choices based on what you see, feel or hear, some of them good choices, others not so good; but God allows you to choose.

Jeremiah 29:11 (NKJV) "I know the thoughts that I think toward you says the Lord, thoughts of peace and not of evil to give you a future and a hope."

While you're trying to figure it out, He already has it figured out. You have your own plans and ideas that seem great. You try your plans and do things your way and are satisfied for a while, but that comes to an end and you are back seeking your purpose in life.

Oh the time you have wasted, just to find yourself unfulfilled, and thinking there has got to be more to life than this.

Matthew 6:33 (NKJV) "Seek first the kingdom of God and His righteousness and all these things shall be added to you."

All the things that make your life fulfilling, satisfying and worth living will be added to you when you first seek God.

Isaiah 55:2 (GNB) "Why spend your money on what does not satisfy? Why spend your wages and yet be hungry? Listen to me and do what I say and you will enjoy the best food of all."

DAY FOUR: TRUSTING GOD'S PLAN

We often make plans regarding our future saying, "I'm going to do this or that." Our plans always seem to be good, but we have no idea of what obstacles may lie ahead. However there is One who DOES know, who also has made plans concerning our present and our future, and has included in His plan how we will manage and/or avoid some obstacles all together.

This is God's Plan, His will for your life.

We can enjoy this wonderful plan He has for us, if we are willing to give up our own plan and trust Him and His plan.

Romans 12:1-2 (GNB) "....because of God's great mercy to us I appeal to you. Offer yourself as a living sacrifice to God, dedicated to His service and pleasing to Him."

This is true worship that we should offer. Do not conform yourselves to the standards of this world, but let God transform you inwardly by a complete change of mind. Then you will be able to know the will of God, what is good and pleasing to Him and perfect."

Oh what wonderful stress free living we would enjoy, if we would but seek God for His plan instead of wanting our own way. We make our plans based on what we get from our 5 senses. God's plan for us is based on truth, fact, what He knows. Now whose plan do you prefer – His or your own?

DAY FIVE: WHO'S IN YOUR COURT?

Today I would like to encourage you to assess who you surround yourself with.

You are the temple of God and God's Holy Spirit dwells in your heart (mind), in your Holy Place. You, as a temple of God, have an inner court where those closest to you in relationship are allowed. Your outer court is the place for those not as close in relationship.

Those whom you allow in your inner court have some influence in your life, including the relationship that goes on in your Holy place. The question you should ask yourself is, do the people in my inner court support, strengthen, or help in building my Holy place relationship?

I Corinthians 16:33 (NKJV) "Do not be deceived, evil company corrupts good habits."

If there are those for whom the answer is NO, might I suggest that you begin moving those people out of your inner court.

Proverbs 4:14 (NKJV) "Do not enter the path of the wicked, and do not walk in the way of evil." Have the right people surrounding you.

Proverbs 2:7-8 (NKJV) "He stores up wisdom for the upright, He is a shield to those who walk uprightly, He guards the paths of justice and preserves the way of His Saints."

Is there anyone you need to remove from your inner court?

DAY SIX: KINDNESS:
AN ANSWER TO A HARD HEART

Psalm 118:24 says "This is the day the Lord has made; let us rejoice and be glad in it."

Today I was thinking of the many challenges we face in our Christian walk. I want to give special attention to those who make it quite difficult to be kind to, and let's pray for them daily (at least one week consecutively). Let's not only pray for them, but for you to be able to demonstrate kindness toward them even when it's difficult. Let's go into this challenge with a mind made up to do some act of kindness toward this individual: compliment them on something they do well, treat them to coffee, or offer to help them with something they may be working on; any kind act that might soften a hard heart. I believe if we make a conscious effort to be kind to all people (even the difficult ones), we would find ourselves and others being kinder. I pray you will join me in this challenge.

II Peter 1: 5-6 "For this very reason do your best, to add goodness to your faith, to your goodness add knowledge, to your knowledge add self-control, to your self-control add endurance, to your endurance add godliness, to your godliness add brotherly kindness, to your brotherly kindness add love."

DAY SEVEN: HE DESERVES OUR PRAISE

Our God is so deserving of our praise.

We attend sporting events, concerts, performances, etc. We hoop and holler over our favorite teams, celebrities, performers and such while our wonderful savior, God the Son who is so much more deserving of our highest praise is usually put on the back burner. We are silent in church during praise and worship; we don't praise Him in our time alone with Him; we don't offer up songs and chants of adoration to Him. Instead, we get right to our needs and wants list, as if sitting on the lap of a heavenly Santa Clause.

Our God has done, is doing and continues to do so many amazing things – for us, to us and through us – and yet we have such difficulty giving Him the praise He deserves. He who looks past all of our faults and sees our needs and not only sees them, but provides them.

God who saw we needed a savior and provided one. The only one who could save us from our sins, stop the works of the devil and put us back in good standing with Him after the Fall of Man.

II Corinthians 5:21 (NKJV) "For He made Him who knew no sin to be sin for us, that we might become the righteousness of God in Him…..Jesus, the sacrificial lamb slain for you and I". Now that's awesome love worthy of praise.

DAY EIGHT: HE HAS A PLAN

Praise God Beloved, for all that He has done, is doing and yet to do. Praise Him for who He is: mighty, awesome, wonderful, faithful, just, merciful…I'm sure you get the picture and could add more to describe how wonderful He is.

He has a plan for your life.

God created you with a purpose.

Jeremiah 29:11 (NKJV) "For I know the thoughts I think toward you says the Lord, Thoughts of peace and not of evil, to give you a future and a hope."

His plan requires: growth, change, transformation, stretching, all which at times can feel uncomfortable. I'm sure you've heard the saying "no pain no gain."

Imagine if clay could talk. I think it would yell and scream and possibly say some not so nice things to the person molding it. You have been created by God for His use. You are yet a work in progress, and like that clay it may take some stretching, pulling, transforming and so on. It may not feel very pleasant at times, but know that God is doing a work in and with you so that He may use you for His glory.

Think about it; you are something very special to God.

He has a special plan and purpose for which He handpicked you. II Corinthians 4:1 (NKJV) "For our light afflictions which is but for a moment, is working for us a far more exceeding and eternal weight of glory."

ACTIVITY

Reflect and answer: How could you sacrifice your time to achieve the growth, change, or transformation you desire?

Purpose: To recognize that you must first make an effort to receive what God has for you.

DAY NINE: CHRISTIAN RESPONSIBILITY

This is the day that the Lord has made; we shall rejoice and be glad in it.

Today I ask you to give attention to your role as believer and your responsibility as an ambassador of Christ.

You, as a Christian, should always desire to represent Christ well in the earth, giving attention to how you treat others, as well as yourself. This includes how you conduct yourself; how you talk (referring to whether you talk negatively or badly of others, yourself or circumstances, or if you use inappropriate language); and what you talk about.

James 1:22 (NKJV) "But be doers of the word and not hearers only, deceiving yourselves."

We do not want to cause others to stumble or push them away from knowing the truth, Our Lord and Savior who is able to save, setting free the captives to this world.

We are to let Christ work in and through us, that men may be drawn to our Lord.

James 5:19-20 (GNB) "Brothers, if any of you wanders away from the truth and another one brings him back again, remember this, whoever turns a sinner back from his wrong way will save the sinners soul from death and bring about forgiveness of many sins."

I challenge you to have someone who will hold you accountable to your responsibility as ambassadors of Christ. One who will be truthful with you and bring correction in love when needed. Let us respect the name by which we are called, and represent Christ well.

DAY TEN: GOD'S FAVOR

I pray that you will be encouraged today.

If there is a matter concerning you, and you are in need of favor; your rent, mortgage, car note is past due, bills piling up with little or no money coming in, you're waiting on a decision concerning your job interview or court case, waiting for health or school test results, company downsizing and waiting to see who stays and who goes....

Whatever it is concerning you today, remember Psalm 5:12 (NKJV): "...with favor you surround him as with a shield." In regards to the person or persons having authority in the matter concerning you, there's Proverbs 21:1 (NKJV) "The King's heart is in the hand of the Lord, like rivers of water He turns it wherever He wishes." I want you to know that God is able and willing to turn the heart of the one that has authority concerning you. You also have power and authority given you by God, over every living thing that moves in the earth. That includes our bodies, bacteria, viruses, etc.

Let's exercise our authority according to God's Word. If it is God's will for you, He is turning it around in your favor.

DAY ELEVEN: HEARING GOD'S VOICE

It is such a wonderful thing to hear from God.

I have not personally heard the audible voice of God, but I have heard the still soft voice that speaks into my conscience many times.

I think that God speaks to you more than you may know. He speaks to you through His Word, through others, dreams and yet other ways. The key is recognizing His voice.

When you know people well through a relationship, you can often recognize their voice even when you don't see them. This also holds true with recognizing the voice of God.

When you know him through personal relationship, by spending time with Him, you become familiar with His voice.

I encourage you to spend time with the Lord, in His Word, in prayer, praise, worship, fellowship with Him. The more time you spend with Him the more aware you will become of Him speaking to you.

John 10:4 (NKJV) "And when He brings out His own sheep, He goes before them, and the sheep follow Him for they know His voice."

DAY TWELVE: NEEDING EACH OTHER

I know you have heard some say, "I don't go to church because the church is full of hypocrites, phony people, and some of the worse sinners".

It is shameful that the world views the church in this way. However, we know that God's concern is our hearts.

1 Samuel 16:7 "For the Lord does not see as man sees, for man looks at the outward appearance, but the Lord looks at the heart."

God knows us and our motives. Psalm 7:9 tells us that "the righteous God tests the hearts and minds."

Modern day scribes and Pharisees will receive an earthly reward from man, and yet be lost. Your focus should be on Jesus, and the development of a relationship with Him.

Hebrews 10:25 (GNB) "Let us not give up the habit of meeting together, as some are doing. Instead, let us encourage one another all the more, since you see that the day of the Lord is coming near."

We all need to be encouraged and as you are taught, your presence also edifies the one who is in place teaching you the word of God. We need one another.

DAY THIRTEEN: LET'S GET TRANSPARENT

It is difficult for people to be transparent with one another. We tend to draw curtains so others can't or won't see what's going on inside. We don't want anyone to know about the mess, turmoil, confusion, unhappiness going on inside ourselves. We put up beautiful curtains, and all types of glass coverings to give the appearance of peace and beauty on the inside.

We don't want to expose the mess that lives inside to everyone because we fear being talked about; people love to talk and gossip about others' mess while covering their own.

Today however, I want to challenge you to a level of transparency with at least one person with whom you can take down the curtains and expose the mess.

This should be a person who will stand and pray with you in the midst of the mess and agree to be present during the clean-up process. This person should be able to hold the waste can while you dump the garbage you have held on to for so long; someone who will be there to see you through to help you find peace to the point of John 14:27, "My peace I give to you, not as the world gives…let not your heart be troubled neither let it be afraid."

Go clean your glass and get transparent.

DAY FOURTEEN: THE GREAT EXCHANGE

How could you ever forget the cross?

Our Lord and Savior, Jesus, went and hung on that old rugged cross. He laid down his life for our sakes. At the cross, He took our unrighteousness, and gave us His righteousness. He took our sick, lame, and diseased bodies and minds that we might receive complete and divine health.

It is here at this old rugged cross that Jesus exchanged our poverty and lack, giving us His abundance of riches. Philippians 4:19 speaks of this when it says, "My God shall supply all your need according to His riches in glory by Christ Jesus."

He exchanged His joy for our sorrow; His wisdom for our foolishness. He exchanged our punishment of death for His eternal life. He took all of our bad, ugly, and worthlessness, to give us goodness, beauty, and value. 2 Corinthians 5:21 states, "for He made Him who knew no sin, to be sin for us that we might become the righteousness of God in Him."

He hung on the cross distorted by shame, guilt, and filthy living, so that we could appear before His Father as clean, pure and holy. It was at this moment of great exchange that His Heavenly Father turned His face from Him, the only begotten Son, to look at us.

Praise the Lord for the great exchange that Jesus made at the cross!

DAY FIFTEEN: RENEW YOUR MIND

I am hoping you are ready to get your mind on your mind. Criminals are arrested, and if found guilty, sent to prison to serve a term of punishment. If punishment allows for release after time served, generally, these individuals can return to society; if not enlightened while in prison, they will return to society with the same mindset (if not worse) than they initially possessed.

How do we expect people to change their actions without first changing their thinking?

Romans 12:2 (NKJV) "And do not be conformed to this world, but be transformed by the renewing of your mind."

Philippians 4:8 (GNB) "Fill your mind with whatever things are good, that deserve praise, things that are true, noble, right, pure, lovely, and honorable."

I can say with much certainty that this is not what the minds of those in prison are being filled with; yet our current system seems to think it somehow rehabilitates these individuals that they may return to society somehow better.

I ask, how?

We are all containers. Containers filled with everything that is put into us daily. Some of that being good, while some not so good. Some of it is just plain old bad.

These are things that have been said, done, and taught to us through various means. All are factors which shape our thinking. Garbage always starts to stink.

Our society desperately needs a mind transformation by the Word of God. When this happens, thinking will change and so will lives.

DAY SIXTEEN: THE COMPANY I KEEP

Today let us give thought to whom we surround ourselves with. Take a look at your life. Are you prospering? Mentally, physically, spiritually, emotionally, financially, educationally, or in any way? Do you motivate, or are you motivated by those whom you surround yourself? I don't mean just talking about what you plan on doing. Do you or your associates put to action any of those plans talked about? Have any of the plans gotten accomplished?

If your answers to most (if not all) of the above questions are NO, then take heed to this saying: "It is insanity to keep doing the same thing over and over again expecting a different outcome."

If you surround yourself with these same people day in and day out, year in and year out all because you have become comfortable and complacent with them you will find yourself satisfied with status quo, mediocre living.

There will be NO growth, NO moving forward, NO prosperity, NOTHING new, better or brighter happening in your life.

HELLO INSANITY!!!!!!!!!!

Come on!!! It's time for a change: in you, in whom you surround yourself, and in your thinking.

Romans 12:2 "And do not be conformed to this world, but be transformed by the renewing of your mind..."

Time to come out of your comfort zone, expand your territory. You and your associates are of no good to each other. Find those whom you all can make each other better.

Proverbs 27:17 "Iron sharpens iron and one man sharpens another."

Let's help make each other better.

24

ACTIVITY

Make a list of the people you consider your friends. Write at least one positive quality that each person adds to you.

Purpose: To identify your true friends. If there is a name for whom you can't produce a positive character trait, you may want to reconsider that relationship.

DAY SEVENTEEN:
ALL IN GOD'S PERFECT TIMING

I'm certain many, like myself, have wondered at times why others are blessed in certain areas and you don't seem to be able to get a breakthrough. You may have prayed days, weeks, months or years without a breakthrough. Then along comes someone who has prayed and trusted God for just a short while, and it seems immediately their breakthrough comes.

God knows us all too well. He knows the what, when, why, where and who to every question. This is why everything He does is perfect. He has all the answers to all of your questions.

He considers your motives for your request, your level of responsibility, whether it is good for you, and the timing.

Ecclesiastes 3:1 (NKJV) "To everything there is a season. A time for every purpose under the Heaven."

God wants to give us the direction we need, so that we may walk in the abundance of all He has supplied for us.

Proverbs 3:5-7 (GNB) "Trust in the Lord in everything you do, and He will show you the right way."

He always knows the right time for everything.

Galatians 4:4 (NKJV) "But when the fullness of time had come, God sent forth His Son born of a woman, born under the law.

He even knew the perfect time to send you a Savior.

DAY EIGHTEEN: THE WORD DOES THE WORK

I want to take time to remind you that God loves you, accepts you, and values you.

This is proven time and time again in the Holy Scriptures.

Romans 5:8 "God demonstrates His own love toward us, in that while we were still sinners, Christ died for us."

This is a serious and true love.

Romans 8:32 "He who did not spare His own Son, but delivered Him up for us all, how will He not also with Him graciously give to you all things?"

God valued you so much He paid for you with the blood of His only begotten Son.

John 17:17 "Sanctify them by your truth. Your word is truth."

You have been hand-picked by God to serve Him. With all your faults and shortcomings, He yet chose you to be His child. He yet chose to clean you up, fix you up, straighten you up, and to build you up with His Word (Jesus) who does all this.

Are you allowing the Word to work? As you study, the Word goes to work.

DAY NINETEEN: STOP ALLOWING IT

God is good.

Have you thought about how many times you have heard that? Do people really believe it, and most importantly do YOU believe it?

When you look at the world around you and see all the violence, prejudice, hate, disrespect, and hear all the profanity, I'm sure you have asked yourself, "How can a good God allow all of this to go on?"

Well the truth of the matter is, it isn't *He* that allows it to go on, but *we* that allow it.

You and I the believer, whom God made in His image as well as gave power and authority over every living thing that moves on the earth.

Genesis 1:2 (AMP) "God said, Let us make mankind in Our image, after Our likeness, and let them have complete authority over the fish of the sea, the birds of the air, the beast, and over all of the earth, and over everything that creeps upon the earth."

You and I have the power and authority to make things happen, to bring change, and being made in His likeness, we are able to speak things into existence.

Are you saying the right things? Are you utilizing your power and authority given to you by your Father, the Almighty God? Or are you sitting idly by while the thief comes and robs you of what was given to you by your Father?

Your Father has given you keys to the kingdom of Heaven, to unlock and lock doors, doors leading to good and/or evil. Are you using your keys?

Matthew 16:19 (AMP) "I will give you keys to the kingdom of Heaven, and whatever you bind on earth, must be what is already bound in

Heaven, and whatever you loose on earth must be what is already loosed in Heaven."

Those known to cause chaos in Heaven were kicked out; it wasn't allowed.

We've got to get serious about what we allow to take place in our lives. We've got to start using our keys. We've got to start binding and loosing.

DAY TWENTY: GROWING UP IN THE WORD

Today we are focusing on spiritual maturity. We as children of God should see signs of growth in our faith walk. There are people who have been a child of God for years, and are yet acting as children in the faith.

There should be greater knowledge, understanding and wisdom concerning the Word of God.

There should be demonstration of godly living, so that others seeking to know, or who are young in the faith may see and learn by examples set by mature believers.

Just as the natural baby needs nourishment for growth, so does a spiritual baby, new in faith.

Spiritual nourishment is supplied through the Word of God. The Word nourishes your spiritual man for spiritual development.

I Corinthians 3:1-2 (GNB) "...and I could not talk to you as I talk to people who have the spirit. I had to talk to you as though you belonged to this world, as children in the Christian faith. I had to feed you milk, not solid food because you were not ready for it and even now you are not ready for it."

Receive the nourishment of God's Word that you may grow.

Luke 2:52 (GNB) "Jesus grew both in body and wisdom, gaining favor with God and man.

Let's get spiritual nourishment and grow daily.

DAY TWENTY-ONE: BLESSINGS OVER YOU

I want to speak blessings over you this day.

Psalm 1:2-3 "To you who delight in the law of the Lord, who meditate on His law day and night, you shall be like a tree planted by the rivers of water, that bring forth its fruit in its season, whose leaf shall not wither and whatever you do shall prosper.

Psalm 5:3 "You, who are godly, know that the Lord has set you aside for Himself."

Psalm 9:9 "For those who are oppressed, the Lord is your refuge in trouble."

Psalm 23:1 & Philippians 4:19 "You shall not live in want, because the Lord who is your shepherd shall provide all your needs, according to His riches in glory by Christ Jesus."

Psalm 34:19 "Though you suffer many afflictions, be secure in in knowing the Lord delivers you out of them all."

Psalm 55:22 "You are not moved or shaken by what you see or experience, because you walk by faith and not be sight and you cast every burden onto the Lord as He is the one who sustains you and will not permit you to be moved."

Proverbs 3:5-6 "As you continue to trust the Lord, even when you don't understand, but acknowledge your need for Him, He will direct your footsteps."

Jeremiah 29:11 "You are His child and He loves you with an everlasting love. He has a wonderful plan for your life that is good and not evil, that will lead you to the bright future you have hoped for."

DAY TWENTY-TWO: PERFECT LOVE

Today, I'd like for us to focus on the wonderful thing called love. There are many who can relate to loving one another with a love that cannot be hindered by distance, time, disagreements, etc., such as the bond between parent and child; siblings; or spouses. Yet, this love is surprisingly imperfect.

We all have the opportunity of experiencing perfect love from our Heavenly Father, who demonstrates His perfect love in a multitude of ways – the giving of His son, Jesus Christ, and the Holy Spirit; his abundance of grace; precious promises to us, and so much more.

Jeremiah 31:3 "...yes I have loved you with an everlasting love; therefore with loving kindness have I drawn you."

If you say you have never known this type of love, know this: Romans 8:38, 39 says, "I am persuaded that neither death nor life, nor angels nor principalities nor powers, nor things present nor things to come, nor height nor depth, nor any other thing created, shall be able to separate us from the love of God which is in Christ Jesus our Lord".

Why don't you rest in God's love?

DAY TWENTY-THREE:
INSECURITY LOOKS LIKE PRIDE

Today's thought is given to insecurity; lacking confidence; inferiority. Many are, or have been, well acquainted with these emotions; there is a remedy for this, and his name is Jesus.

John 8:36 "Therefore if the Son makes you free, you shall be free indeed."

Praise God, you can be free! One would never think self-centered to be associated with these feelings; however, being self-centered has many faces. When we give so much attention to ourselves, and what we think others think about us; how we look; what we have; doubting our abilities; we are being self-centered.

When we are so busy focusing on self that we leave little to no room to focus on God. When we are too busy depending on self, we give little to no opportunity to depend on God. We are too busy looking at, and relying on our own abilities; we neglect Philippians 4:13, "I can do all things THROUGH CHRIST who strengthens me."

Doing things through Christ does not mean we have to be the best, have the most, or go the furthest. It just means we are able to accomplish our goal, and we can do it without envy; we can recognize and celebrate those who are better at something than we are.

Proverbs 16:18 "Pride goes before destruction, and a haughty spirit before a fall."

DAY TWENTY-FOUR: KNOWING TRUTH

Today, I would like you to turn your attention to the words used to describe our wonderful Lord God in Genesis 24:27, "Praise the Lord God of my master Abraham who has been faithful and true keeping His promise to my master".

The servant of Abraham calls God "faithful and true" because He had proven Himself to the servant.

God has proven Himself over the centuries to be reliable and trustworthy. He operates only in truth, in word, and deed. Isaiah 55:11 says, "So shall my word be that goes forth from my mouth. It shall not return to me void, but shall accomplish what I please, and it shall prosper in the thing for which I sent it."

If you are born again, you have recognized and experienced some of God's truth, like the sealing of the promised Holy Spirit. Yet some seem to have difficulty believing all of God's word as truth, and therefore don't experience all of His truth.

I pray that you and I will arrive at Psalm 51:6, "Behold you desire truth in the inward parts and in the hidden parts; You will make me to know wisdom."

When we are at this place of truth, we really experience God's promises.

DAY TWENTY-FIVE: DESTINATION

Believers often speak of the goodness of God, and the unbeliever often asks "How can a supposedly good God send people to hell?"

The truth of the matter is....God doesn't send people to Hell.

Matthew 18:11 (NKJV) "For the Son of Man has come to save that which is lost"

People send themselves to Hell. Isaiah 53:6 (GNB) "All of us like sheep that were lost, each of us going his own way, but the Lord made the punishment fall on Him, the punishment all of us deserved."

We all have the same opportunity of salvation, to acknowledge the truth. Acts 20:34 (GNB) "...I realize that it is true that God treats everyone on the same basis."

Yet there are those who choose to live their own way, regardless. Romans 1:18-19 (GNB) "God's anger is revealed from heaven against all sin and evil of people whose evil ways prevent the truth from being known. God punishes them, because what can be known about God is plain to them, for God Himself made it plain". [If this has in some way pricked you or made you feel otherwise unsettled, I pray that it is your heart, pricked open to receive truth.]

ACTIVITY

Reflect on the choices that you have made in your life. If you were to die tomorrow, based upon those actions, do you think your destination would be Heaven?

Purpose: To determine whether your lifestyle needs improvement.

DAY TWENTY-SIX:
THE POWER OF COMMUNICATION

Do you know the power of communication?

I am sure if asked to give thought to how much communication you have experienced in your lifetime, it would be best to just leave it at, "a lot". There are so many ways of communicating: spoken language; body language; sign language; facial expressions; written communication, and the list goes on and on.

Messages are being relayed in all of your communication, but have you ever given much attention to *how* you communicate with others?

Generally, are you pleasant in your conversation, drawing others to you? Or, do you find that people try to avoid communicating with you because of your unpleasantness?

Ephesians 4:29 (GNB) advises us, "Do not use harmful words, but only help words, the kind that build up and provide what is needed, so that what you say will do good to those who hear you.

What we say to people, as well as how we say it, can make or break a relationship; practicing how to communicate with others is very important. Always be mindful that you are representing God; you are the ambassador of the King of Kings, the Lord God Almighty – I am sure you want to represent Him well. You are representing Him not only in your deeds, but also your words.

Proverbs 31: 26 (GNB) "A good man's words are a fountain of life, but a wicked man's words hide a violent nature."

So remember, if you don't have something good that will benefit the hearers, it is best not to say anything at all. The Lord does everything with good reasoning. He gave us two ears and one mouth so that we may hear and listen twice as much as we talk.

DAY TWENTY-SEVEN:
WORKING IT OUT FOR MY GOOD

I hope that I am able to clear up the misconception of many, that a Christian, believer, follower of Christ (whatever your term) only experiences hardships, trials, tribulations or sufferings if not living right before God.

John 16:33 informs us that "in the world you will have tribulation, but be of good cheer, I have overcome the world."

In whatever you may be going through, let Psalm 27:1 be your confession, "The Lord is the strength of my life, of whom shall I be afraid?"

The strength of your life can, will, and has already helped you through many of life's storms. Know that in our suffering, which is often painful, God is still working it out for good.

Hebrews 2:10 "For it was fitting for Him, for whom are all things and by whom are all things, in bringing many sons to glory, to make the captain of their salvation perfect through suffering."

It is often during our suffering seasons, out of desperation that we seek, even run to cling to God the most.

DAY TWENTY-EIGHT:
WORLD IN NEED OF HEALING

Today my heart is heavy, not just for our nation, but for the world; as we are getting further and further away from the word of God.

It says in 2 Timothy 3:16 that "all scripture is given by God, and is profitable for doctrine, for reproof, for correction, for instruction in righteousness."

To profit is to gain, to have something added to you, yet our society is not experiencing profit. People are losing so much: their homes, families, jobs, respect, faith, hope, even their lives.

We need help. We all need Jesus. We all need to cry out to the Lord every day; seek Him every day; thank Him every day for what He has already done, for what He is doing, and for what He is yet to do.

2 Chronicles 7:14 "If my people who are called by my name would humble themselves, and pray, and seek my face, and turn from their wicked ways, then I will hear from heaven and forgive their sin and heal their land."

Our world is so badly in need of healing. Let's meditate on this word today; humbly examine ourselves, seek His face, repent, and pray for self and others that our land may be healed.

DAY TWENTY-NINE: YOU AND ME LORD

I pray all is well.

I would like if you would give your attention to relationships today…more specifically, your relationship with the Lord.

When we make up our minds to allow God the Son to be our Savior and Lord, we are choosing to be in a relationship with Him; and like with any other relationship, it takes the involved parties to do their part to make the relationship work.

I can assuredly say that Jesus has done, is doing, and will continue to do His part. He will never forsake you in the relationship; His love for you is everlasting. He has already provided all that you will ever need to live an abundant life. Now, what about you and your part?

Your part is very big in making this all work. He wants you to trust Him. To trust that everything He does concerning you is always for your good. Proverbs 3:5 gives us to "trust in the Lord with all your heart."

Without you believing in Him, your relationship can't work. Hebrews 11:6 reminds us, "but without faith it is impossible to please Him."

He also wants your honor and respect. Psalm 111:10 says, "The fear of the Lord is the beginning of wisdom." This speaks not of being fearful of Him, but of reverencing Him for who He is.

He desires for us to love and obey Him. John 14:15 states, "If you love me keep my commandments."

How do you think your relationship is going?

DAY THIRTY: YOU ARE GETTING BETTER

Today, let's praise God for another day, another opportunity to be better at loving Him; one another; and ourselves.

2 Corinthians 3:18 (GNB) "All of us then, reflect the glory of the Lord with uncovered faces and the same glory coming from the Lord, who is the spirit who transforms us into His likeness in an ever greater degree of glory."

The events of your past, whether good or bad, God has a way of working them out and using them for good. Romans 8:28 encourages us, "And we know that all things work together for good to those that love God, to those who are the called according to His purpose."

Whether mistakes you or others have made, from which you may have learned a hard lesson or which may have caused great pain, you experience the healing process because of God's abundance of love, grace and mercy. It is generally at your most painful, trying times, that you really seek after the Lord, allowing Him to work on the scars of your past. But, with each scar, at each level of the healing process, you are being transformed.

Romans 12:2 "And do not be conformed to this world, but be ye transformed by the renewing of your mind, that you may prove what is that good and acceptable and perfect will of God."

Thank God that you continue to make it through every obstacle, trial, and pain, seeing the opportunities in all of it; growing stronger, wiser, more patient, kinder, and all that the Lord is developing you to be.

DAY THIRTY-ONE:
YOU ARE SPECIAL AND LOVED

I am praying that as you read and meditate on these scriptures today you will become in tune with how special you are to God, and how very much He loves you.

Jeremiah 1:5 "Before I formed you in the womb I knew you. Before you were born I sanctified you." In this verse, God's words are spoken to Jeremiah the prophet about you. God not only wanted, but planned and made a way for you to be here. No matter through whom or how, just know that God wanted you here in the earth.

He brought us forth through our parents, and according to His plan, we are here. He set us aside for Himself to be instruments of use for His glory.

God says about you, what He said about Jesus before performing any miracles, "you are my son/daughter, in whom I am well pleased (Mark 1:11).

The Father wants you here, and made you unique, for a special purpose. He has a wonderful plan for your life because He loves you.

DAY THIRTY-TWO:
ARE YOU READY FOR IT?

I hope you have gotten off to a good start today, giving praise to the Lord God Most High, being mindful that even when things don't work out the way you plan or expect, you know the omniscient God.

Things do not work according to our plan, but His plan. There are often times that things don't work out as we expect, which may be because our timing is off; but He does everything at just the right time.

Jeremiah 29:11 reminds us, "God has a plan that is good and not evil, a plan for a bright future in which you have hoped." It is your job to trust in the fact that He loves you, and has your best interest at heart.

At times, we become anxious for things to happen to, or for us, which we are not really ready to receive. Philippians 4:6 says "be anxious for nothing, but in everything by prayer and supplication, with thanksgiving, let your request be made known to God."

Your Heavenly Father delights in giving you the desires of your heart. In all of His grace and mercy, He is careful not to give you more than you are able to handle. If you have something that draws you away from Him, or might be a stumbling block in your spiritual growth, it could simply mean that you are not ready for it yet, and He knows it.

Those desires could be good, but not good for you at that time; such as a person wanting to get married, but unsure of how to care for themselves, or a person wanting their own business, but has difficulty managing their personal life.

Luke 12:48 helps us prepare by letting us know, "everyone to whom much is given, of him much is required."

So I pose this question, are you really ready for what you are asking?

DAY THIRTY-THREE:
CORRECTION IN THE BODY

In my reading and meditation of scripture, I felt lead to give attention to bringing correction to the body of Christ. Yes, as believers we have our moments of not behaving like Christ. Romans 3:23 even gives us to know, "for all have sinned and fall short of the glory of God."

However, it is of great concern for those who yet practice sin without thought. 1 Corinthians 5:12 "for what have I to do with judging those also who are outside? Do you not judge those who are inside?" This verse is referring to awareness of wrongdoing, and our responsibility in bringing correction to our brother or sister when we see them doing something that causes harm.

Sin is always harmful. It is out of love for that individual that you bring correction so that they may not continue to bring harm to themselves or others.

John 15:12 says, "Love one another as I have loved you." If you see someone you love causing harm, you should intervene to stop the damage. This is what God did for us; He saw us harming ourselves through sin, leading to death, and sent Jesus to intervene and stop the damage. And He did better than that; not only did He stop it, but He repaired it so we could be better. Jesus took our old damaged lives to make them better than they were before.

When you see a need for intervention, first give the matter to God in prayer. If need be, seek out Godly counsel. There may be occasion when you are not the person to bring the correction because the individual will not receive it from you. Also, timing as to when and how to approach the person is important. However, what is most important is that correction is brought so that the member of the body may repent and be restored.

DAY THIRTY-FOUR: BELIEVING GOD

Today's focus is on faith in action.

Mark 11:24 "Therefore I say unto you, whatever things you ask when you pray, believe that you receive them and you will have them."

It doesn't matter how it looks, how you feel about it, if you pray believing. You shall have what you ask for according to God's Word. When you actually believe, your actions and attitude will demonstrate your believing.

Though we don't see it yet, we know it's already done, and that it will be made manifest to us. If you are believing God for a job, have your clothing cleaned, pressed and ready to start work. If believing God for a child, start picking out baby names. Plan your schedule so that it will accommodate your new addition. Maybe it won't be a child from your own body, but a child that needs to be loved and YOU are the one able to give that love.

Let me give you a few prayer pointers:
- Don't ask God for another's husband or wife, as we are commanded not to covet.
- Don't ask God to give you a million dollars when you can't well manage twenty-five dollars, as we are commanded to be faithful over a few things.
- Don't pray expecting based on your time limit. God's timing is always perfect.
- Pray according to God's Word. Pray believing and receive.

Jeremiah 1:12 (NKJV) "...for I am watching over My Word to perform it."

ACTIVITY

Read Matthew 6:9-13.

Purpose: To demonstrate how to align your prayer with God's will for your life.

DAY THIRTY-FIVE: LOVE WALK

Everyone wants to be loved and we are all loved.

John 3:16 says, "For God so loved the world that He gave His only begotten Son, that whosoever believes in Him should not perish but have everlasting life."

Romans 5:8 reiterates this notion, "But God demonstrates His own love toward us, in that while we were still sinners, Christ died for us."

He didn't die for us because we were good, deserving, or even because we loved Him, but it was His love for us as stated in 1 John 4:19, "We love Him because He first loved us." Love is our tool for winning souls, loving people through the Christ in us.

When we acknowledge and receive the truth that Christ died for our sins, was buried and resurrected on the third day, we received Him. His spirit, the one that raised Him from the dead, came to live within us.

We have the power to love like Jesus loves, even those who seem unlovable; however, it is a process. We need to practice loving others, being mindful that He is here to help throughout the process.

1 John 4:7 "Beloved, let us love one another, for love is of God and everyone who loves is born of God and knows God."

Let us continue our journey on a love walk.

DAY THIRTY-SIX: READY FOR WORSHIP

I pray that today, you will develop an attitude of worship.

Worship is simply acknowledging God with excellence at all times. We can worship the Lord every day, all day. The Lord delights in our worship, and in knowing that we are mindful of Him.

In our daily worship to the Lord, we give the best of ourselves in behavior, attitude, performance, finances, and time, among other things. Colossians 3:23 encourages, "whatever you do, do it heartily, as unto the Lord and not to men."

We engage in worship when what we give is fresh and enthusiastic, our best. We were created to worship God.

Revelation 4:11 "You are worthy, O Lord, to receive glory and honor and power; for You created all things, and by Your will they exist and were created."

God is the reason that we live, and we should live to worship Him.

DAY THIRTY-SEVEN: READY TO CONQUER

Psalm 107:1 "Oh give thanks to the Lord, for He is good, for His mercy endures forever."

You have been given everything you need to see victory in your life, your family, your community, and the world. So, as it states in 2 Timothy 3:17, "that the man of God may be complete, thoroughly equipped for every good work."

Ephesians 6:13 advises us, "Therefore take up the whole armor of God that you may be able to withstand in the evil day." Daily, you must put on your helmet of salvation; knowing who and whose you are in Christ Jesus. You are to put on the breastplate of righteousness to guard your heart, so not to be tainted with the poisons of this world. Hold up your shield of faith, which will protect you from the fiery darts of deceit thrown at you by your enemies. Forget not the belt of truth that holds you up so that you can stand in truth. Use the sword of the Spirit (the word of God), to chop down your enemies. Cover your feet with the preparation of the gospel of peace, so that wherever you go, you bring peace. You must stay alert and prepared for the enemy's attack.

Remain strong and bold enough to stand up for righteousness, even when it's not popular; do not compromise truth, and do not waiver.

When you stand firm in truth, you walk in victory. You shall experience what it is to be more than a conqueror.

DAY THIRTY-EIGHT:
STRAIGHT FROM THE HEART

Is your life ministering the goodness of God to those around you?

There are people who quote Bible scripture that they have either heard or read, but do not take to heart, much less apply to their life. James 1:22 tells us, "but be doers of the word, and not hearers only, deceiving yourselves."

The world doesn't need religious people, but people who sincerely desire to know the Lord God, and obey what He says. God is not as interested in what we do (He does not want us to sin under any circumstance, however), but why we do the things we do, which comes down to a matter of the heart. Proverbs 27:19 "As in water face reflects face, so a man's heart reveals the man."

You may be able to convince another that your intentions are right when they are not, but God cannot be deceived.

Psalm 7:9 "Oh let the wickedness of the wicked come to an end, but establish the just. For the righteous God tests the hearts and minds."

Let's stay focused on loving God, others, and ourselves out of a pure heart daily, with conscious sincere efforts of pleasing God in word and deed from the heart.

DAY THIRTY-NINE: JESUS, SAVIOR AND LORD

Psalm 103:1 "Bless the Lord, O my soul and all that is within me, bless His holy name."

We have so much to be thankful for; thankful for Jesus Christ, the relationship with Him; what He did on Calvary, taking away our sins by dying on the cross.

God gave Jesus, His only begotten Son, to be the sacrificial lamb for the forgiveness of sin, and give life everlasting. He died to be our Savior, and rose to be our Lord. 2 Corinthians 5:15-18 states, "He died for all, that those who live should live no longer for themselves, but for Him who died for them and rose again. Now all things are of God who has reconciled us to Himself through Jesus Christ, and has given us the ministry of reconciliation."

Jesus wants to not only be our Savior, but our Lord. He wants us to trust Him with our lives; allowing Him to direct us, and control every part of our lives so that we may live the abundant life that is promised to God's children. He is the only way into the family of God. "I am the way, the truth, and the life. No one comes to the Father except through me" (John 14:6).

My prayer is that you will give close attention to the most important relationship you will ever have; that you will be truthful with yourself when answering this question: Have I made Jesus Christ my Lord and Savior?

The relationship with Jesus will positively affect every relationship you will ever possess.

DAY FORTY: IT'S IN THE GRACE

Psalm 68: 19 "Blessed be the Lord, who daily loads us with benefits, the God of our salvation."

As children of the Lord God Most High, we have new mercy each day; we are loved unconditionally; we have abundance of grace for all the day; and we get these things anew each day the Lord gives.

His grace covers all. Grace is what cannot be earned, nor is it deserved. It is all the goodness of God that is available to us by faith in Christ Jesus.

We have joy, healing, peace, deliverance, redemption, forgiveness, sanctification, righteousness because of grace and what Jesus did on the cross.

There was once a commercial for spaghetti sauce where the slogan was "it's in there" a reference to all of the good ingredients. The same can be said about God's grace. All of the goodness of God mixed in grace, and packaged in Jesus Christ.

Psalm 34:8 encourages us to partake in the goodness, "Oh taste and see that the Lord is good, blessed is the man who trusts in Him."

God has supplied everything we will ever need in His grace.

DAY FORTY-ONE: HEALING IN MY MIND

Praise God for all that was accomplished on the cross!

Today, I pondered on the state of mind, both before and after salvation; or what I call the pre-salvation and post-salvation mindset.

In the pre-salvation state, the mind streams with dark, wicked unpleasant thoughts, which according to Webster's dictionary, is a type of illness. Our sinful nature makes us sufferers of mental illness, plagued by wicked thoughts.

Romans 3, verses 10 and 23 (respectively) state, "There is none righteous, no not one. For all have sinned and fall short of the glory of God."

Jesus paid for our salvation, deliverance, justification, redemption, and healing with His blood on Calvary's cross. The stripes He bore in his flesh were endured so that one day we would be able to be healed. When we receive Christ into our hearts, we have available to us all that He paid for, including a sound and healthy mind.

Romans 12:2 "And do not be conformed to this world, but be ye transformed by the renewing of your mind."

Glory to God, our thought process can be as bright as we want it to be.

DAY FORTY-TWO: KNOWING TRUTH

Today, let's turn our attention to the words used to describe our wonderful Lord God in this passage: "Praise the Lord God of my master Abraham who has been faithful and true keeping His promise to my master".

The servant of Abraham calls God "faithful and true" because He had proven Himself to the servant.

God has proven Himself over the centuries to be reliable and trustworthy. He operates only in truth, in word, and deed. Isaiah 55:11 says, "So shall my word be that goes forth from my mouth. It shall not return to me void, but shall accomplish what I please, and it shall prosper in the thing for which I sent it."

If you are born again, you have recognized and experienced some of God's truth, like the sealing of the promised Holy Spirit. Yet some seem to have difficulty believing all of God's word as truth, and therefore don't experience all of His truth.

I pray that you and I will arrive at Psalm 51:6, "Behold you desire truth in the inward parts and in the hidden parts; you will make me to know wisdom."

When we are at this place of truth, we really experience God's promises.

DAY FORTY-THREE:
MAKING GOD YOUR FIRST PRIORITY

Today we are focusing on our priorities.

You often think of priorities from a natural perspective: family, career, education, finances, etc.; a way of organizing our lives based on levels of importance of the people and things in it.

Looking at and organizing life from a spiritual perspective should have your priorities organized a little bit differently.

Matthew 6:33 (NKJV) "But seek first the kingdom of God and His righteousness and all these things shall be added to you." The Christian Life is not to be treated as if it is a recreational activity; living right should be your way of life. Being a Christian isn't what we do; it's who we are, how we live.

Romans 8:9 (NKJV) "Trust in the Lord with all your heart, and lean not on your own understanding. In all your ways acknowledge Him, and He shall direct your paths."

The Lord is interested in every area of your life. When you make Him your number one priority, He will give you godly wisdom in organizing everything else in your life.

ACTIVITY

Write down your spiritual priorities.

Purpose: To ensure that you are on track to executing God's plan for your life.

DAY FORTY-FOUR: IT'S A LOVE THING

As I think on love, I think of a child who knows he is loved, and how this child responds to that love.

I also think about the love a husband has toward his wife. Ephesians 5:25 "Husbands love your wives, as Christ loved the church and gave Himself up for her."

God, in all of His infinite wisdom knew that when love is given, the recipient would respond favorably; we all desire to be loved. It is this desire that draws us to our Heavenly Father. 1 John 4:19 says, "We love Him because He first loved us."

When we come into the revelation of the truth that God loves us unconditionally, with absolutely no strings attached, it is then that we are set free from trying to earn God's love; because the truth is, no matter what we do we could never earn it. His love is a free gift available to us all; the only thing we must do is receive it.

God has given us proof of His love by giving His only Son, Jesus when we had no desire for Him. "But God shows and clearly proves His love for us by the fact that while we were still sinners, Christ died for us" (Romans 5:8).

That is awesome love! Jesus died for us that we might have life, and that more abundantly. Abundant in love, joy, peace, health, mercy, grace, and all that makes life wonderful.

Roman 8:32 "He who did not withhold or spare His own Son but gave Him up for us all, He will also with him freely and graciously give us all things."

We live in a society that is starving for this love thing.

DAY FORTY-FIVE: THE GOOD PLAN

Psalm 139:14 "I am fearfully and wonderfully made. Marvelous are Your works."

He knew you even before you were formed in your mother's womb, and He still knows you. He knows all about you, your thoughts, dreams, secrets, success, and failures.

Psalm 139:1 says "Lord you have searched me and know me."

Praise be to God, even with all that He knows about you, He still says, "I choose you to be mine". No, you didn't choose Him; He chose you. You were part of His plan, and the plan that He has for your life is good.

DAY FORTY-SIX: LET IT SHINE

Matthew 5:14 "You are the light of the world. A city that is set on a hill cannot be hidden."

The Lord refers to us as the light of the world, and being such, we are to bring light into dark places. We are to be as a light bulb; when someone enters a dark room and the light is turned on, they that have entered the room are able to see better.

We are the bulbs connected to the power source that generates light. We can't be afraid to let that light shine wherever we go. Matthew 5:16 encourages us, "Let your light so shine before men, that they may see your good works and glorify your Father in Heaven."

If you asked Christ into your heart, you now have the light in you. So let it shine outwardly for all to clearly see they too have a choice; either remain in the dark, or come into the light so they may also shine.

DAY FORTY-SEVEN:
QUALITY TIME WITH THE LORD

I want to take this time to encourage you, in making time with the Lord a priority so that you may develop your relationship with your Lord and Savior.

Make time for talking with Him.

Make time for sitting still in quietness that you may hear when He speaks to you.

Make time for not just the reading of his word, but for studying it.

You will see that as you seek him with diligence, He will reward you with revelation knowledge and understanding of his word. Hebrews 11:6 tells us, "He is the rewarder of those who earnestly and diligently seek him."

In your quality time with the Lord, you will find that you are nourished, renewed and transformed in your mind.

We often spend too much time digesting the garbage that the world dishes out daily, via television, radio, other technology. We have a free will to make choices, not having to accept and eat all the garbage that the world serves. This free will gives the choice of which meal we want to spend time feeding on - the healthy daily bread offered by our Heavenly Father, or the other junk food offered by the world.

DAY FORTY-EIGHT: DAILY SOUL FOOD

John 1:1 "In the beginning was the word, and the word was with God, and the word was God."

I pray that you are encouraged to dig into the word of God daily, as it is truly food for your soul. It is nourishment to keep your spirit man strong and healthy.

God's word is daily bread provided by our Heavenly Father, in the form of the Bible, and in the form of his only begotten son Jesus.

When you keep your eyes fixed on Jesus and the example he gave on how to live, you are spiritually strengthened to go on a little further with him. John 6:35 "Then Jesus declared, I am the bread of life. Whoever comes to me will never go hungry and whoever believes in me will never be thirsty."

There are times you may find yourself craving something you don't have in your refrigerator or cupboards. You try satisfying the craving with other things you have available but nothing satisfies; this is what happens with our inner man or soul, it craves to be satisfied, and the only thing that will satisfy your soul's craving is Jesus.

Once you receive him, the craving is gone.

Jesus satisfies your inner craving that is meant to be filled by him and only him. If you try and satisfy this soul craving with anything else, it will only be a temporary fix; the craving will return. Nothing else will do.

DAY FORTY-NINE:
HAVE YOU READ THE INSTRUCTIONS

"God is not a God of disorder but a God of peace" (1 Corinthians 14:33).

God is of order and he wants for us to live a life of order.

He has given us a book of instructions for living a life of order…have you read the book? It is the Holy Bible.

It says in 2 Timothy 3:16 "All scripture is given by inspiration of God, and is profitable for doctrine, for reproof, for correction, for instruction in righteousness."

The Bible is our manual for living a holy and orderly life.

1 Peter 1:16 instructs us, "be holy, because I am holy."

These are things which are important to God and therefore should be important to us. It is when we do not read the book of instruction that we experience the most difficulty.

The same holds true when you buy something and don't really know how to put it together. You should read the assembly instructions first, because without doing so, you usually find yourself frustrated trying to figure it out. You may possibly experience even more repercussions for not following the given instructions.

This is why we go through many of life difficulties; we don't read the book of instructions for life. When we operate and act outside of God's order by not following His instructions, we find ourselves experiencing pain and suffering.

Yes the Bible does say that we will experience these things.

Our Omniscient God knows our weakness and frailties. He also knows that we will not follow all of the instructions by the book, His holy word.

Praise God, that He takes those moments of us doing things our own way and turns them into learning experiences. He doesn't hold them against us.

To live the life God has prepared for us, when need to follow His instruction book.

DAY FIFTY:
HEARING AND LISTENING TO THE FATHER

God often communicates with us, but some do not recognize His voice because of the lack of time spent developing that much needed intimate relationship with the Father. This time allows us the ability to distinguish our Father's voice.

Yet others don't know His voice because He is not their Father. John 20:4 (AMP) says, "When He has brought His own sheep (His children) outside, He walks before them and the sheep follow Him because they know His voice."

There are others who have become so preoccupied with "stuff" that they pay little to no attention to the Father's direction, instruction, or correction, and therefore suffer much distress.

Life could be more satisfying for those who heed 2 Corinthians 20:5 (AMP) "Refute arguments, theories, and reasoning, and every proud and lofty thing that sets itself up against the knowledge of God, and we lead every thought a purpose away captive into the obedience of Christ."

Are you hearing and listening to what the Father is trying to tell you?

DAY FIFTY-ONE: CHASTENED BY LOVE

How about some real talk?

In my thoughts today are people that do the right thing, but for the wrong reasons. We will call this being "nicety". The deed itself is good, but the motive for doing the deed is wrong.

I am sure that like myself, you can think of times you did something nice for someone because it would somehow benefit you, but all the while you murmured and complained. This is what I refer to as being nicety.

If you in all truth know that this was once you, I hope in your spirit, you also experienced conviction for such behavior. When you are convicted of sin by the Holy Spirit, it is simply God correcting you as his child. Revelation 3:19 (NKJV) says, "As many as I love, I rebuke and chasten. Therefore be zealous and repent."

God in all of his wonderful fatherly love, chastens you his child because he loves you, and wants you to love others as he loves you. From a pure heart.

DAY FIFTY-TWO: FROM GLORY TO GLORY

Praise God Saints!

Today as you meditate on the Lord, give attention to where the Lord has brought you regarding your life's journey.

When you think of the person you used to be and look at the person you are today, I hope your heart is filled with gratitude for the work the Lord has done, is doing and yet to do in you.

II Corinthians 3:18 (NKJV) "But we all, with unveiled face, beholding as in a mirror the glory of the Lord, are being transformed into the same image from glory to glory, just as by the Spirit of the Lord."

No, you are not by any means perfect, and may be a long shot off, but praise God, He finishes everything that He starts.

The enemy likes nothing more than to remind us of the person we once were and tries to convince us that we have not, nor can we ever really change. I want you to know that the devil is a liar, and there is no truth in him. He wants you to feel the shame and guilt of your past, but is it just that: the past; it is all behind you. You are now looking and moving forward, going from glory to glory.

ACTIVITY

Make a list of past mistakes that still plague you.

Pray and ask God to forgive you and release the burdens of carrying those sins.

Burn the list.

Purpose: To alleviate the stress and guilt of holding on to the past.

DAY FIFTY-THREE: WHILE THERE IS TIME

Come on in where you can find safety, peace, joy, strength, health, and a whole lot more. Come on in and you can bring others too; there is plenty of room for all to come.

I welcome you into the Secret Place.

Psalm 91:1 (NKJV) "He who dwells in the secret place of the Most High shall abide under the shadow of the Almighty." It is here in the Secret Place that you find everything you need.

The Secret Place is in the arms of the Father. Jesus, who is the light of man, the only begotten of the Father, brings us all to the Secret Place when we are ready and willing. It is the light of Jesus that casts the shadow of the Father, and in this shadow is a place of protection and provision.

The door is open for everyone who will come, but there will one day come a time when the door will close. It will not close because there is no more room. There is just a time period set by the Father for all to come.

It is only the Father who knows when the time periods end and when the door will close.

Matthew 24:36 (NKJV) "But of that day and hour no one knows, not even the angels of Heaven, but My Father only."

There is much room for others to come, please bring them while there is time.

DAY FIFTY-FOUR: ARE YOU A WORSHIPPER?

Praise God, here you are again with another day to worship the Lord.

Matthew 2:2 (NKJV) says "Where is He who has been born King of the Jews? For we have seen His star in the East and have come to worship Him."

I pray that as you go through out your day, you will worship the King of Kings and Lord of Lords in all that you say and do.

The Lord delights in your worship, and hears the prayers of the worshipper that does His will.

John 9:31 "Now we know that God does not hear sinners, but if anyone is a worshipper of God and does His Will, He hears him."

The Lord God can be worshipped wherever you are, at any time. You are simply acknowledging and reverencing the presence of Almighty God at all times. With this being said, your talk and actions will reflect in your worship.

Psalm 4:24 lets us know, "God is Spirit, and those who worship Him must worship in Spirit and Truth.

DAY FIFTY-FIVE: HE WILL SEE YOU THROUGH

Psalm 39:1 (NKJV) "I will bless the Lord at all times, His praise shall continually be in my mouth."

We should keep this always in our mind, no matter what is going on in our lives, or around us. The Lord never promised that the Christian life would be easy, or without trouble; in actuality, He said the opposite: Psalm 34:19 "Many are the afflictions of the righteous, but the Lord delivers him out of them ALL."

Matthew 7:14 states, "…narrow is the gate and difficult is the way which leads to life and there are few who find it."

You can, however, be confident that the Lord has your back. No matter what the storm, trial, or test, He wants you to make it through, to pass, so that we may continue to move forward.

I Corinthians 10:13 "…no temptation has overtaken you except such as is common to man, but with the temptation will also make the way of escape, that you may be able to bear it."

He is a way maker, and He has made a way to get you through the storms that come your way.

Bless the Lord.

DAY FIFTY-SIX: NAKED AND UNASHAMED

Genesis 3:10 "I heard your voice in the garden, and I was afraid because I was naked, and I hid myself."

Today, come standing naked and unashamed.

In the beginning Adam and Eve had been in the garden naked without feelings of fear or shame, until sin came to mankind (disobeying God); now fear and shame was present with man.

We often try and hide shame. We put on many masks of emotions, attitudes, character, etc. for fear of exposure.

MEMO: God knows who's behind the mask! He knows of the shame. He also has a remedy for that fear and shame, just as He had a remedy for Adam and Eve.

God provided a covering. Genesis 3:21 says, "…also for Adam, and his wife, the Lord God made tunics of skin and clothed them.

He provided a covering for our shame also…Jesus. His shed blood covers and cleanses of shame.

John 1:9 (NKJV) "…if we confess our sins, He is faithful and just to forgive us our sins and to cleanse us from all unrighteousness."

If you are covering up shame (dysfunctional family, inferiority, etc.), God knows and has forgiven you. Now forgive yourself and or others, and be free to stand naked and unashamed.

DAY FIFTY-SEVEN:
THE WORD'S POWER TO CHANGE

Praise God for His written and living word.

John 1:1 "In the beginning was the word, and the word was with God and the word was God." This Word has in it the power to bring change.

As we not only read, but study the word, it transforms us, our way of thinking.

Our actions are controlled by how and what we think.

II Timothy 3:16 states, "All scripture is profitable for doctrine, for reproof, for instruction in righteousness."

The Word of God does all of this, but yet many don't get into a routine of studying the Word of God.

Many prefer to get advice, correction, and instruction from the world. While seeking professional counsel isn't opposed (doctors, psychiatrists, etc.), let's seek God's professional counsel; knowing the Source of power can change you, your life, and your situation.

The Living Word was the Word manifest in the natural in the form of Jesus Christ, who gave his life for us.

The Word changes things.

DAY FIFTY-EIGHT: TAKING IT BACK

Are you ready for battle?

The enemy has people on the run from their communities, families, responsibilities, commitments, and from God.

Satan is taking territory that your Heavenly Father has given you. It is time to take it back!

It is heart breaking to see the enemy ravage what the Lord has given us to enjoy, while we sit back fearful and powerless. It is time to say ENOUGH!!!

Satan has been allowed to have control of our belongings, both natural and spiritual, far too long; and it is we who have allowed Him control. It is known that anything Satan controls he destroys: our communities, families, marriages, relationships, finances, minds, bodies, anything.

I Peter 5:8 tells us, "Because your adversary the devil walks about like a roaring lion, seeking whom he may devour."

The enemy may be *like* a roaring lion, but he's not a lion; he only has the roar. He may even throw a few fiery darts, but we have something greater.

Jesus our Lord and Savior came to stop the works of the devil. He took back the keys to the kingdom and returned them to us, but we seem to forget we hold the keys.

Let us stand up, stand strong in the Lord, knowing who we are in Christ Jesus.

Let's take back our stuff!!!

DAY FIFTY-NINE:
THE LORD'S BENEFIT PACKAGE

Praise God for His abundance of love, grace, and mercy.

It is such a wonderful thing to be a child of God.

Psalm 68:19 (NKJV) "Blessed be the Lord who daily loads us with benefits, the God of our salvation."

You as a child of God have so many wonderful benefits available. You have eternal life, no longer awaiting the death sentence, the punishment you deserved; instead you receive all the goodness that you did not, nor can ever earn, also included in your "Saved by Grace Package".

I Corinthians 2:16 (NKJV) "....we have the mind of Christ" (you can think like Christ!)

Proverbs 16:9 (NKJV) "A man's heart plans his way, but the Lord directs his steps" (direction from the Lord)

Psalm 23:1 (NKJV) "The Lord is my shepherd I shall not want" (all your needs met)

Isaiah 53:5 (NKJV) "But He was wounded for our transgressions, He was bruised for our iniquities. The chastisement for our peace was upon Him, and by His stripes we are healed" (freedom from not just sin, but a sinful life, complete healing from head to toe, inwardly and outwardly, and peace from every torment).

Let me just add a couple other benefits; I am sure you can come up with more.

Psalm 91:7 (NKJV) "A thousand may fall at my side and ten thousand at my right hand, but it shall not come near you." (Divine protection)

It's all available free to you, because it has already been paid for by Jesus, with His blood.

I don't know about you, but it makes me shout HALLELUJAH!!!
We have only put a dent in our benefit package and there is enough for all.

Give our Lord some praise for all His benefits.

ACTIVITY

List some of the many benefits you have received.

Purpose: To make you aware of the abundance of blessings God provides.

DAY SIXTY: IN CLOSING

Genesis 1:26 (AMP) "God said, 'Let us make mankind in Our image, after Our likeness, and let them have complete authority over the fish of the sea, the birds of the air, the beasts, and over all of the earth, and over everything that creeps upon the earth."

This is such an awesome scripture telling you who you are; you were made in the image of God. When God said in OUR image, He is speaking of the three-part Trinity: God the Father, God the Son, and God the Holy Spirit - The Divine Planner; the plan; and the worker of the plan.

You have so much greatness inside of you as a child of God. You even have an instructor to help you along your way. Psalm 32:8 declares, "I will instruct you and teach you in the way you should go; I will guide you with My eye."

You know what else you have? You have been given the authority to do it.

Go ahead, exercise your God-given authority. You can accomplish the plan because you have an ever present help.

www.ingramcontent.com/pod-product-compliance
Lightning Source LLC
Chambersburg PA
CBHW062027040426
42447CB00010B/2169